Live. Love. Lick.

Live. Love. Lick.

The Yorkie Tea Holiday Etiquette Guide

AUTHOR:

The Yorkie Tea Society

CONTRIBUTORS:

🐾 *Original Paw-scriptions by the Yorkie Tea Council*

🐾 *Translated (with care and treats) into Human Language by the Society's Recording Secretary*

Recording Secretary's Note:

The Yorkie Tea Society's holiday musings have been faithfully transcribed from their paw-scribed correspondence and tea-time dictations. Any inaccuracies are likely due to biscuit crumbs in the typewriter.

Live. Love. Lick.

Dedicated to the original members of the *Yorkie Tea Society*—
Theadora (2010–2022) and **Charles** (2012–2025) —
whose love, sass, refined palates, and impeccable sense of occasion inspired it all.

And to every dog who graciously allows humans into their story, making our families — and our hearths — immeasurably warmer.

Live. Love. Lick.

A Welcome from the Yorkie Tea Society

At *Yorkie Tea*, we believe life is best served with lace, laughter, and a little mischief — and of course, as many Yorkies as possible. Our council of finely coiffed companions has gathered to share their wit and wisdom, ensuring your holiday season is as polished as silver — and twice as shiny. Consider this guide your invitation to sip the sass, savor the charm, and remember that in the grand theater of life… Yorkies always steal the spotlight.

Live. Love. Lick.

Table of Contents

Live. Love. Lick.

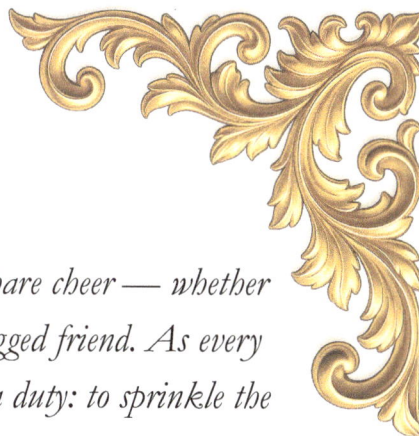

Dearest Reader,

The holidays are a time to fling open one's paws and share cheer — whether with your favorite human or a suitably civilized four-legged friend. As every well-bred Yorkie knows, our noble lineage comes with a duty: to sprinkle the world with elegance, polish, and just the right dash of sass.

What follows is not mere advice, but a carefully curated treasury of Yorkie-isms — etiquette so refined it could balance a teacup on its head, yet so practical it will carry you through the chaos of carols, crumbs, and ill-placed tinsel.

Remember, my dears: the true answer to "Who's a good girl?" or "Who's a good boy?" is always the same — those who mind their manners.

Yours in tea, tales, and tiny triumphs,
Lady Theadora Pawthorne

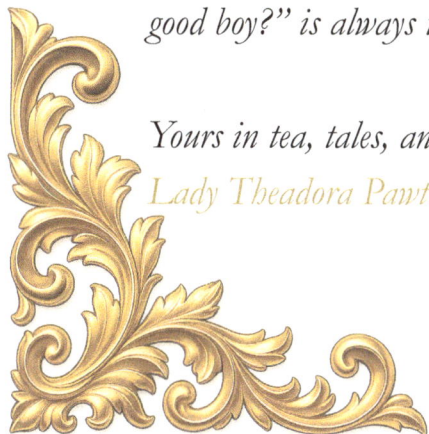

🐾 RULE #1: HOSTING WITH PAWS & GRACE
Lady Theadora Pawthorne

"A true hostess never forgets to place a cushion for her most distinguished guest… especially if said guest weighs fewer than seven pounds."

My dears, the holidays are no time for chaos. A proper hostess — whether two- or four-legged — must embody serenity, sparkle, and just the right amount of sass. The most treasured moments, as any Yorkie will attest, arrive in the most petite packages: a velvet bow, a well-timed cuddle, a crumb of shortbread.

Set the Stage: A hostess must craft an atmosphere that whispers luxury, never sloppiness. Velvet cushions, fluff-lined corners, and cozy nooks for intimate tête-à-têtes set the tone. Every guest deserves comfort — and no Yorkie should ever be relegated to bare hardwood. Velvet cushions are the minimum, though tartan throws may suffice in emergencies.

Welcoming: Each guest deserves warmth, whether in polished shoes or muddy paws. A polite sniff at the doorway and a gracious tail wag suffice. Should someone forget to remove their boots, resist scolding; a dainty pawprint across their coat offers a more elegant reminder.

Ambiance: Ambiance is everything. Let the air carry faint notes of roast turkey, with music that is festive yet refined. Seventeen rounds of Jingle Bells is an insult to good breeding; far better the gentle jingling of a collar bell.

Nibbles & Noshes: Tiny paws deserve petite portions. A steady flow of one-bite delights prevents crumb trails, overstuffed stupors, or late-night battles with coats and harnesses. Always send guests home with treat bags half-full rather than spirits wholly depleted — a useful mantra for both hosting and life.

Remember: hosting is not about perfection, but presence. A home brimming with laughter, candlelight, and perhaps a squeaky toy under the sofa will always outshine a silent house of polished silver. With grace, a hostess not only sets the table — she sets the tone for the season.

A Hostess's Horror List

- Forgetting to provide cushions for guests under seven pounds.
- Serving kibble without garnish.
- Allowing mismatched bows at the table.
- Leaving squeaky toys visible (they must be tucked away until *after* dessert).

🐾 RULE #2: MANAGING HOLIDAY STRESS
Sir Charles Barkington

"Time is best measured in meals, not minutes."

Greetings, dearest companions. Sir Charles Barkington at your service. Once a scrappy fellow of modest circumstance, now (through rescue and refinement), I stand a gentleman of... what's the word? Repu-taste-shun. Yes, that.

The holidays, I must confess, test even the most seasoned aristodog. Between jingling bells, glittering baubles, and Aunt Mildred's fruitcake, one's composure can wobble like a pup on polished parquet. But despair not. Allow me to present three guiding maxims, carefully cultivated through trial, error, and the occasional overturned gravy boat:

1. "An occupied mouth spares a frazzled mind."
Noise, relatives, and jingling contraptions can overwhelm the constitution. A steady flow of hors d'oeuvrays (or "floor snacks," as the common folk say) restores serenity and prevents one from growling at in-laws.

2. "If the eggnog flows too freely, a nap beneath the tree is not disgrace but gallantry."
Sometimes the finest contribution one can make is tactical retreat — curled nobly upon the velvet tree skirt. To the casual observer it may look like dozing; in truth, it is stress management at its most chivalrous.

3. "Every ornament is a test of character."
The baubles beckon, the tinsel twinkles, temptation abounds. A true gentleman resists—until no one is looking. Then—and only then—a single paw-bat, modest and controlled, may be permissible in the interest of "holiday quality assurance."

In summation, dear reader: I am no flawless noble. I am, at heart, a fellow who relishes meat scraps, velvet cushions, and inclusion at the table. That, I humbly propose, is the marrow of holiday grace: presence over perfection, crumbs over criticism, and dignity — mostly intact.

A GENTLEMAN'S NAP LOCATIONS, RANKED

1. **Velvet tree skirt** – optimal balance of softness and visibility to food.
2. **Under the dining table** – access to crumbs, though risk of stampede.
3. **In the coat pile** – indulgent, but beware eau de mothball.
4. **Parlor sofa** – too obvious, too contested.

Live. Love. Lick.

🐾 RULE #3: THE SCIENCE OF THE HOLIDAY TABLE
Professor Q.T. Snugglesworth

"Yorkies increase holiday enjoyment by no less than 98%."

Dearest pupils, as the world's foremost authority on Yorkie etiquette (a title bestowed upon me unanimously by myself), I present to you a series of carefully researched, peer-reviewed insights for optimal holiday dining. [1]

Restraint: A well-bred guest does not beg, paw, or bark for scraps. Such primitive tactics are best left to breeds of…lesser refinement. Today's modern Yorkie practices dignified restraint, securing morsels through intellect, timing, and gravitas.[2]

Placement: Location is everything. When the faint perfume of roast fills the air, one must not remain idle. Trot forward with scholarly purpose, nudge aside bystanders if necessary, and secure the prime position: directly beneath the roast. Empirical evidence confirms that a Yorkie so positioned is 78% more likely to acquire leftovers with dignity intact.[3]

Proximity: Beyond roast strategy, maintain visual and tactile access to one's human. Holidays test even the most resilient of two-leggeds, who inevitably collapse under the weight of fruitcake, eggnog, and family drama. They require steady emotional support in the form of chin nuzzles, ankle warmth, and, when conditions demand, full lap occupation. Multiple studies (all authored by me, naturally) conclude that Yorkies increase holiday enjoyment by no less than 98%.[4]

In conclusion: placement is power, posture is prestige. Those who grasp this truth shall ascend the table's hierarchy. Those who do not… shall fetch the crumbs.

[1] Snugglesworth, Q.T., "On the Self-Evident Supremacy of Yorkies," Proceedings of the Royal Yorkie Academy, Vol. 1.
[2] Snugglesworth, Q.T., "Dignity Over Drool: A Modern Approach to Table Manners," Journal of Canine Refinement, Vol. 4.
[3] Snugglesworth, Q.T., "Crumbs as Currency: A Quantitative Analysis," Annals of Roast Studies, Vol. 7.
[4] Snugglesworth, Q.T., "Lap Occupation as Emotional Regulation in Humans," Journal of Festive Psychology, Vol. 3.

Etiquette Equations for the Holiday Table

Researched and peer-reviewed by Q.T. Snugglesworth

Optimal Roast Yield (ORY):

ORY = (Proximity to Roast × Duration of Stoic Stare) ÷ Number of Labradors Present.

Conclusion: Position is everything. Labradors skew the results unfavorably.

Crumb-to-Snack Ratio (CSR):

CSR = Floor Crumbs Collected ÷ Seconds Since Dropped.

A Yorkie must act within 1.3 seconds for maximum crumb retrieval efficiency.

Human Attention Span (HAS):

HAS = (Volume of Guest Conversations × Glasses of Eggnog Consumed) ÷ Presence of Yorkie Under Table.

Reminder: Stay within patting radius to maintain optimal HAS.

Holiday Happiness Index (HHI):

HHI = Yorkie Presence × Frequency of Chin Nuzzles^2.

My findings, peer-reviewed by myself, unequivocally prove that Yorkies increase holiday joy by at least 98%.

🐾 RULE #4: GIFTING ETIQUETTE
Miss Gigi "Cupcake" Lickleigh

"Too sparkly for the naughty list."

Oh, hello darlings — it's me, Gigi. Or, as most people know me, Cupcake— because apparently "Gigi" wasn't fabulous enough. (Humans simply cannot resist downgrading our elegant names into syrupy nicknames: "Pumpkin," "Snuggle Muffin," or, heaven forbid, "Sir Wigglepants." We permit it, of course. Why? Because frankly, we are irresistible.)

Now, to the matter at paw: gifts. The holidays are the season of giving — and no one gives quite like a Yorkie. We give sparkle, cuddles, and, occasionally, decorative tooth marks on the corners of unattended parcels.

The Joy of Unwrapping
If there is paper, there must be shredding. That's law. But do it with flair: a dainty paw here, a polite tear there, followed by a full terrier frenzy. When the parlor is blanketed in festive confetti, tilt your head, widen your eyes, and voilà — you are no longer a menace, you are a memory maker.

Stockings & Surprises
Stockings are not "out of reach." They are invitations. Opportunities. Daring feats of acrobatics! The sight of me, on hind legs, wobbling toward treasure like a pint-sized ballerina, is the sort of spectacle humans will replay endlessly. And if I tumble into the fireplace poker stand? Divine slapstick. Bonus points if it's filmed, set to Mariah Carey, and captioned with at least ten crying-laugh emojis.

The True Gift
Never forget: we are the real presents. The toy's squeaker will wear out, the ribbon will fray, but your Cupcake — your Pudding, your Baby Boo, your Fluffy McSnugglekins — is eternal. My antics, my cuddles, my star power — these are the treasures no money can buy.

So, unwrap with gusto, darlings. Shred, prance, leap, repeat. And when all is chaos, sit prettily in the center of the room and remind them: the best gift is always the Yorkie.

🐾 RULE #5: CONVERSATION TOPICS AT THE FEAST
Sir Charles Barkington

"Etiquette is easier on a full stomach."

Polite repartee is the crown jewel of civilized dining. Alas, I've learned this the hard way. Last year, I attempted to discourse on the weather but, in a lapse of judgment, ate the centerpiece instead. My punishment? Exile to the bedroom until dessert. Mortifying.

Thus, let us establish some guardrails so that one's words secure favor (and scraps) rather than disgrace.

Safe Topics
- Treats (an evergreen subject).
- Travel ("why yes, I've journeyed from kitchen to sofa—exhausting but enlightening").
- Turkey (preferably with tasting notes).
- Velvet cushion preferences.
- Seasonal bows and their proper placement.

Faux Paw Topics
- Cats (divisive, dangerous, and dreadfully dull).
- Squirrels (too political).
- Vacuum cleaners (the horror speaks for itself).
- Aunt Blanche's mystery casserole.
- Holiday waistline expansion of one's humans (an unkindness too far).

Do not blurt out "WHEN IS DINNER?" at full volume. It lacks refinement (however heartfelt).

Do secure a pre-feast nibble. Etiquette, as I always say, is far easier on a full stomach. It equips one with the fortitude to engage in spirited debate—say, the longevity of squeaky toys or the proper chew-resistance of rawhide.

In sum, remember: conversation is not merely chatter, it is strategy. Speak with grace, avoid faux paws, and always position yourself near the roast. If you slip, well—flash your most endearing look, lazy tongue encouraged. It has saved me many a time.

🐾 RULE #6: DRESS CODES & HOLIDAY FASHION
Miss Gigi "Cupcake" Lickleigh

"The star on top? It's me."

While at finishing school in Paris — the prestigious *Académie de Sit, Stay, et Paw-litesse* — I learned that true style is not worn, it is embodied. Yes, my simple humans thought it was a "dog training school." Quelle naïveté. It was a runway. A stage. A proving ground for the art of entrance-making.

And holidays, my loves, are our season. Sequins. Satin. Velvet. Glitter. And bows — oh, the bows! To humans, a ribbon is mere décor. To us, it is destiny. I often recall the words of the great Coco Chewnel: "If it crinkles, shred it. If it sparkles, wear it."

A bow perched just so atop my silky mane? Iconic. A satin ribbon trailing behind me as I prance through the parlor? Performance art. Nothing says "holiday cheer" like a Yorkie turning the living room into a catwalk while the humans squeal, "Oh, Gigi!" — phones out, capturing every strut for posterity (and their socials).

Now, darlings, a word of warning: indulgence must be timely. A poinsettia collar in December is très chic. In January? Tragic. Sparkle with abandon while the season allows, for when the clock strikes midnight on a new year, the same ensemble becomes a faux paw more grievous than chewing the hem of your human's new cashmere scarf.

And remember: whether you choose prêt-à-porter or haute couture, nothing fits a Yorkie better than charm, sass, and unapologetic self-importance. Wear that, and you will never go out of style.

22

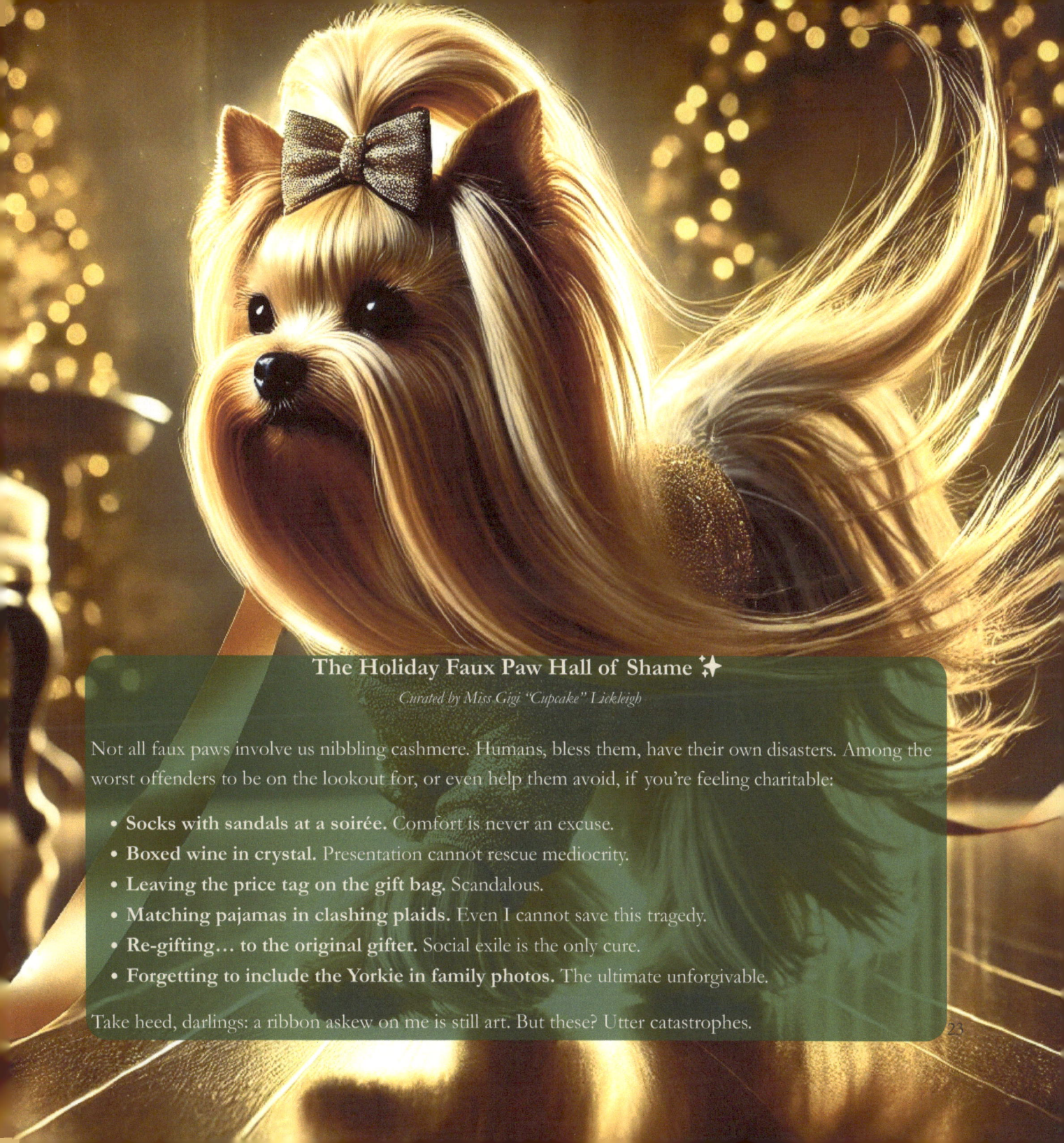

The Holiday Faux Paw Hall of Shame ✨

Curated by Miss Gigi "Cupcake" Lickleigh

Not all faux paws involve us nibbling cashmere. Humans, bless them, have their own disasters. Among the worst offenders to be on the lookout for, or even help them avoid, if you're feeling charitable:

- **Socks with sandals at a soirée.** Comfort is never an excuse.
- **Boxed wine in crystal.** Presentation cannot rescue mediocrity.
- **Leaving the price tag on the gift bag.** Scandalous.
- **Matching pajamas in clashing plaids.** Even I cannot save this tragedy.
- **Re-gifting… to the original gifter.** Social exile is the only cure.
- **Forgetting to include the Yorkie in family photos.** The ultimate unforgivable.

Take heed, darlings: a ribbon askew on me is still art. But these? Utter catastrophes.

🐾 RULE #7: TEATIME TRADITIONS
Lady Theadora Pawthorne

"Where there is warmth, wit, and a wagging tail, there is always decorum."

My dears, one cannot properly conclude a holiday without a steaming pot of tea and a companionable cuddle by the fire. After all, the grandest soirées are not judged by their centerpieces—eaten or intact—but by the contented sighs that follow them.

Be it Earl Grey for the humans or chicken broth for the more discerning palate, tea is more than refreshment. It is ritual. It is theater. It is where civility and scandal meet over a shared saucer.

Stories of bauble temptations, tales of turkey negotiations, even whispers of squirrel sightings all find their way into the cup. It's the hour when we tease Sir Charles about Gravyboatgate and indulge our dear Professor's insistence that "Q.T." stands for "Quintus Thaddeus" rather than the suspiciously similar "cutie." All in good fun, of course—with a knowing twinkle and impeccable posture. After all, what is Yorkie Tea if not equal parts refinement and repartee?

Humans, too, are part of the ritual—and how fortunate they are. They brew, we supervise. They chatter, we judge. They pour the tea, and we settle into their laps to make it sweeter than sugar. Without a Yorkie at one's side, the ceremony is merely pleasant. With us, it becomes art.

There is, of course, etiquette even here: sip delicately, share cushions generously, and if one must doze, do so gracefully upon velvet rather than snoring beneath the canapé tray. As my Charles is fond of proving, charm excuses nearly everything—but only if one remembers to wipe one's paws.

And so, as the final log crackles and the last crumb is savored, let the evening end as it should—with warmth, wit, and just enough sparkle to remind everyone that the tea may cool… but the Yorkie commentary never does.

Live. Love. Lick.

Blessings from the Yorkie Tea Council

The time has arrived, dear reader, for the Council of Yorkie Tea to bid you adieu. You have trotted with us through wreaths and ribbons, feasts and faux paws, naps beneath trees and scraps beneath tables. We trust you now see the holidays as we do: not simply a season, but a stage — and every Yorkie, the star of it.

Before we part, each of us offers a final blessing — a pawprint of wisdom to tuck into your holiday heart as you navigate the delights (and occasional disasters) of the season:

- 🐾 **Lady Theadora Pawthorne:** *"Sip the sass, but always with grace."*
- 🐾 **Sir Charles Barkington:** *"A crumb shared is a crumb doubled."*
- 🐾 **Miss Gigi 'Cupcake' Lickleigh:** *"It's a Yorkie world — tie your ribbon and own it."*
- 🐾 **Professor Q.T. Snugglesworth:** *"The data confirms: bigger is just… bigger."*

And so, dear reader, we raise our cups — and our paws. May your holidays be merry, your ribbons impeccable, your biscuits abundant, and your dignity… mostly intact.

Until next season — **live, love, lick, as only a Yorkie can.**

Join the Yorkie Tea Community

Darlings, the holidays may fade, but *Yorkie Tea* is forever. It is not merely a season — it is a society. A year-round celebration of sparkle, etiquette, ribbons, and revels. And naturally, we insist you join us.

Why, you ask?

Because here, every day is cause for celebration. We sip, we shred, we prance, we ponder — and, of course, we spill the tea. From behind-the-scenes glimpses of the Council in session to exclusive interviews with other distinguished breeds (yes, even the Pomeranians and Poodles), your cushion at the table awaits.

Your Invitation:
• Follow our antics, wit, and wisdom on social media — where humans, as they should, post us in our best light.
• Share your own Yorkie's ribbons, mischief, and holiday faux paws with the hashtag #YorkieTea.
• Raise your teacup — porcelain or paw-shaped — and join a community where the sparkle never fades.

Your exclusive invitation awaits at yorkietea.com.

Because, after all, it's a Yorkie world — we're simply letting the humans live in it.

Yorkie Tea - Holiday Playdate Menu

(Peer-reviewed by Professor Q.T. Snugglesworth, Ph.Dog)

Every proper holiday fête requires a menu. Here, the Yorkie Tea Council has compiled a quartet of festive delicacies—safe, delightful, and certain to dazzle both palate and paw. Do remember: always consult your trusted veterinarian before introducing new treats, and serve in moderation. (Even Sir Charles will attest that excess crumbs invite a most undignified mid-feast nap.)

🧀 Duchess's Delightful Biscuit Bites

A savory morsel suited for distinguished palates and special occasions. Opt for low-fat, low-sodium cheese and serve sparingly — grace, after all, lies in moderation (and in crumb-free paws).

Ingredients

- 1/2 cup finely shredded low-fat cheddar or part-skim mozzarella
- 3/4 cup oat flour (blend rolled oats)
- 1 large egg
- 2–3 Tbsp water, as needed

Directions

1. Heat oven to 325°F / 165°C. Line a tray with parchment.
2. Mix cheese, oat flour, and egg. Add water a little at a time until a soft dough forms.
3. Roll small 3/4-inch balls; press gently with a fork for ridges.
4. Bake 15–18 minutes until set. Cool fully. Store chilled up to 5 days.

Professor's Note: Cheese is an optional variable: test a pea-sized nibble first for lactose sensitivity. Elegance fades when tummies rumble.

Live. Love. Lick.

✦ Gigi's Vegan Sparkle Rounds (Vegan)

A plant-based showstopper that turns any snack into a spotlight moment. Rich with peanut butter aroma and full of flair — no artificial glitter required: your Yorkie is the sparkle.

Ingredients

- 1/2 cup pure pumpkin
- 2 Tbsp natural peanut butter (unsalted, xylitol-free)
- 1 Tbsp ground flax + 2 Tbsp water (rest 5 min)
- 3/4 cup oat flour

Directions

1. Heat oven to 325°F / 165°C. Line a tray with parchment.
2. Stir pumpkin, peanut butter, and flax mixture until smooth.
3. Fold in oat flour to a soft dough. Pinch 1-teaspoon pieces; shape into petite coins.
4. Bake 16–20 minutes until set. Cool completely before prancing the runway.

Professor's Note: Sparkle is metaphorical. However, a flawless sit-and-stay increases treat allocation by an observed 22%.

🎩 Sir Charles's Turkey & Sweet Potato Bites

The minutes at family gatherings may stretch into miles, but a steady cadence of these hearty morsels will sustain even the most genteel guest — right up to the moment you see them off with a courteous ankle-nip farewell.

Ingredients

- 1 cup cooked ground turkey (lean, unseasoned)
- 1 cup mashed sweet potato
- 1 egg
- 1/2 cup oat flour

Directions

1. Preheat oven to 350°F (175°C).
2. Combine turkey, sweet potato, and egg in a bowl.
3. Stir in oat flour until mixture holds together.
4. Form into small bite-sized balls and place on a baking sheet.
5. Bake for 20 minutes until firm.
6. Cool before serving.

Professor's Tasting Notes: "Protein content satisfactory. Temptation level: extreme."

❄ Professor-Approved Cottage Cream Nibbles (Diabetic-Friendly)

A low-sugar, protein-forward finale to round out the feast with scholarly restraint. As always, confirm with your veterinarian for diabetic dogs — peer-reviewed, of course.

Ingredients

- 1/2 cup low-fat, plain cottage cheese (low-sodium)
- Optional: 2 Tbsp plain Greek yogurt (unsweetened)
- Silicone mini-mold or ice cube tray

Directions

1. Blend cottage cheese (and yogurt if using) until smooth.
2. Spoon into mini molds; freeze 60–90 minutes until set but not rock-hard.
3. Pop out 1 mini nibble and let soften 30 seconds before serving to toy breeds.

Professor's Note: Evidence suggests even those with sugar restrictions may indulge—responsibly. Observe individual response and timing with insulin/meal schedule.

Bon appétit, dear companions.
Whether savory, sweet, or somewhere delightfully in between, these morsels will keep tails wagging and spirits bright. And should a crumb (or two) fall to the floor — well, Sir Charles insists that's merely efficient hosting.

Safety First
Use only plain, unseasoned ingredients. Avoid onions, garlic, chocolate, raisins, alcohol, xylitol, and high-fat scraps. Introduce any new treat gradually, start with tiny portions, and keep treats to ≤10% of daily calories. For diabetic or medically sensitive dogs, always confirm timing, dosage, and portion size with your veterinarian before serving.

From the Yorkie Tea Council
These recipes are original adaptations, lovingly crafted and taste-tested in the distinctive Yorkie Tea voice.

www.ingramcontent.com/pod-product-compliance
Lightning Source LLC
Chambersburg PA
CBHW061050090426
42740CB00002B/104